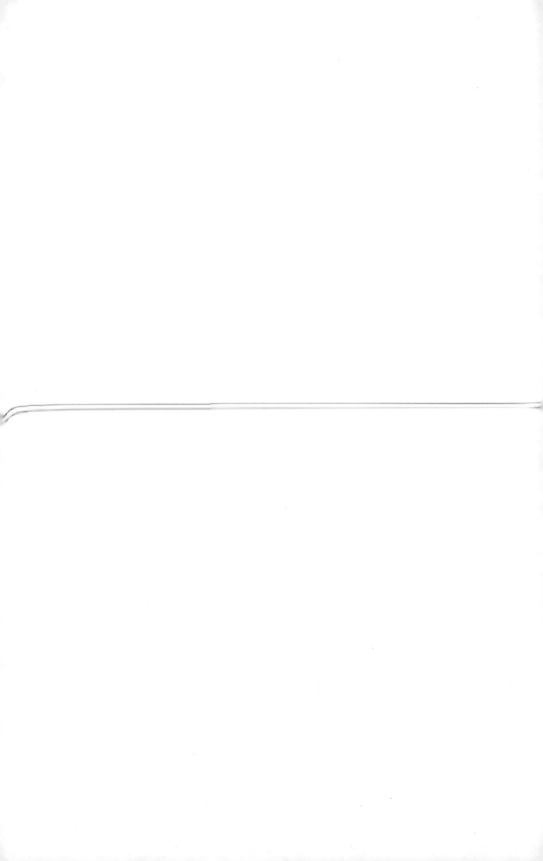

Harriet Beecher Stowe
and *Uncle Tom's Cabin*

Susan Dudley Gold

Cavendish Square
New York

Published in 2016 by Cavendish Square Publishing, LLC
243 5th Avenue, Suite 136, New York, NY 10016

Library of Congress Cataloging-in-Publication Data

Gold, Susan Dudley.
Harriet Beecher Stowe and Uncle Tom's Cabin / Susan Dudley Gold.
pages cm. — (Primary sources of the abolitionist movement)
Includes bibliographical references and index.
ISBN 978-1-50260-528-3 (hardcover) ISBN 978-1-50260-529-0 (ebook)
1. Stowe, Harriet Beecher, 1811-1896. Uncle Tom's cabin. 2. Stowe, Harriet Beecher, 1811-1896—
Criticism and interpretation. 3. Uncle Tom (Fictitious character) 4. Slavery in literature.
5. Race relations in literature. I. Title.

PS2954.U6G65 2016
813'.3—dc23

2015007637

Editorial Director: David McNamara
Editor: Amy Hayes
Copy Editor: Cynthia Roby
Art Director: Jeffrey Talbot
Senior Designer: Amy Greenan
Senior Production Manager: Jennifer Ryder-Talbot
Production Editor: Renni Johnson
Photo Researcher: J8 Media

The photographs in this book are used by permission and through the courtesy of: Universal History
Archive/UIG via Getty Images, cover; Hulton Archive/Getty Images (top), Peter Newark American
Pictures/Bridgeman Images (bottom), 5; Schlesinger Library, Radcliffe Institute, Harvard University/
Bridgeman Images, 8; Public domain/Southworth and Hawes/File:William Lloyd Garrison by Southworth
and Hawes, c1850.png/Wikimedia Commons, 10; Library of Congress, 11; Public domain/H. Seymour
Squyer/File:Harriet Tubman by Squyer, NPG, c1885.jpg/Wikimedia Commons, 13; Transcendental
Graphics/Getty Images, 15; North Wind Picture Archives, 16; Public domain/File:Harrietjacobsreward.
jpg/Wikimedia Commons, 17; Fotosearch/Getty Images, 19; Picture History/Newscom, 20; Public
domain/File:Theodore Dwight Weld.jpg/Wikipedia, 21; Everett Historical/Shutterstock.com, 22; Public
domain/File:Shadrach Minkins for sale.jpg/Wikimedia Commons, 26; Look and Learn/Bridgeman
Images, 27; MEPL/Alamy, 28; File:Alanson Fisher - Harriet Beecher Stowe - Google Art Project.jpg/
Wikimedia Commons, 32; Library of Congress, 35; File:Queen Victoria.jpg/Wikimedia Commons,
35; Public domain/Jeremiah Gurney & Sons/File:Charles Dickens by Gurney, 1867.jpg/Wikimedia
Commons, 37; Library of Congress, 39, 41; North Wind Picture Archives, 43; Library of Congress, 46–47;
*AB85.H7375.A863n, Houghton Library, Harvard University/File:Houghton AB85.H7375.A863n -
Grand Jubilee Concert.jpg/Wikimedia Commons, 48; Jenkins/Getty Images, 50.

Printed in the United States of America

CONTENTS

A Nation's Conscience

Abraham Lincoln—so the legend goes— once greeted Harriet Beecher Stowe, the author of *Uncle Tom's Cabin*, with the words: "So you're the little woman who wrote the book that started this great war."

Standing under five feet (1.5 meters) tall, this middle-aged mother of seven, a New England preacher's daughter and biblical scholar's wife, described herself as "a mere drudge with few ideas beyond babies and housekeeping."

Yet Stowe, who never lived in the South and never witnessed slavery beyond a quick visit to a Kentucky **plantation**, managed with her pen to rally millions of people around the world against the institution that enslaved human beings. Certainly other factors played major roles in creating the rifts that led to the American

Civil War. But Stowe's emotional tale of slavery in the South focused international attention on the plight of slaves and stirred sympathy for them as people. Historians have described *Uncle Tom's Cabin* as the book that awakened a nation's conscience.

In the decades leading to the Civil War, the United States broiled with controversy. The question of slavery divided the nation as the North and South jockeyed for power. The South's economy depended on slave labor to work the plantations and harvest cotton, tobacco, rice, and other money-producing crops. In 1800, nearly all the nation's slaves—94 percent—lived in the South. Their labor, considering slaves worked at least sixty hours a week year-round, would have been worth more than two hundred billion dollars a year. (That amounts to trillions of dollars in today's values.)

Slaves had to work long hours in sweltering conditions picking cotton on plantations in the South before the Civil War.

Northerners, who had few slaves, nevertheless benefited from the South's trade. Shipbuilders, textile factories, bankers, and others in the North made money from Southern plantations dependent on slavery. For that reason, many in the North tolerated the use of slaves in the South.

Allowing more states with slaves to join the **Union**, however, threatened the balance of power between North and South. Under the US Constitution as written at the time, slaves could not vote, but they counted when figuring the number of representatives to Congress each state was allotted. Five slaves were equal to three white men in the count for representatives and presidential electors. That meant states with slaves had a larger proportion of representatives per voters than **free states** did. Though some Northerners opposed the expansion of slavery on moral grounds, others did not want to admit new **slave states** because it gave voters in the South more power.

Abolitionists, those who opposed slavery, gained ground as slaves escaped from cruel Southern masters and told their stories. It became harder for Northerners to ignore the vicious brutality and abuses linked to what many referred to as the South's "peculiar institution." Desperate slaves staged rebellions that brought further attention to their miserable conditions. Although the revolts failed, they spread fear throughout the South and led to tighter restrictions on free blacks as well as slaves.

For decades, the nation's obsession with slavery swirled in a cauldron of injustice, cruelty, brutality, and fear. Stowe's powerful story of America's slaves—first published in 1851—stirred the pot to boiling.

Evil Slavery

Harriet Beecher came from an influential New England family of educators and ministers. The sixth of eight surviving children of Lyman and Roxana Foote Beecher, Harriet was born in Litchfield, Connecticut, in 1811. She was only five when her mother died. Her stepmother, Harriet Porter, added three more children to the family.

An impressive speaker and popular religious leader, Lyman Beecher, a Presbyterian and Congregational minister, became well known for speaking out against society's ills. All seven of Harriet's brothers followed their father into the ministry. Her older sister, Catharine, founded a school for young women, the Hartford Female Seminary, where Harriet attended as a teen. She later taught at the school, which taught women advanced studies and prepared them for a career in teaching.

The remarkable Beecher family, around 1859. Standing, from left: Thomas, William, Edward, Charles, and Henry. Seated, from left: Isabella, Catharine, Lyman (father), Mary, and Harriet.

Lively Conversations

As a young girl, Harriet grew up in a busy household filled with talk about religion, politics, and literature. Family and friends read poetry and classical books aloud and acted in plays written to entertain those gathered at the parsonage. Catharine, who helped raise Harriet after their mother's death, was especially skillful at writing humorous pieces on the household's antics. An uncle who traveled the world as a sea captain shared his adventures in faraway cultures. Students at the nearby Litchfield Law School—the first such school in the nation—boarded at the family's Connecticut home, and Harriet witnessed many a debate at mealtimes. The lively conversations around the dining room table taught Harriet the skill of expressing herself well.

At age eight, Harriet joined her sisters as a student at Sarah Pierce's Litchfield Female Academy. While there she studied literature, geography, science, mathematics, and other topics typically taught at schools for young men. Students were also schooled in religion and morality. Harriet began writing essays every week. By the age of twelve, her writing was polished enough to be featured at a school exhibition. Her essay titled "Can the immortality of the Soul be proved by the light of nature?" won her father's praise—a fact that made Harriet especially proud.

At the Hartford Female Seminary, Harriet took courses in ethics, Latin, and Greek as well as the subjects she had studied at Miss Pierce's school. American society at the time expected young women to become wives and mothers. Few opportunities existed for women who wanted a career. Nevertheless, with Catharine as a role model, the school instilled in its young female students the goal of living useful, independent lives. After graduation, at age sixteen, Harriet taught writing at the school, a job she held for five years.

While Harriet attended the seminary in Hartford, Harriet's father, stepmother, and younger siblings moved to Boston. Lyman Beecher, at the height of his career, accepted a prestigious post as minister of Boston's Hanover Street Church. His booming voice exhorted parishioners to take action on behalf of one cause or another. His passionate appeals brought new members to the church and sparked a revival of faith among Bostonians.

One of the new church members was William Lloyd Garrison, who would later gain fame as a leader in the **abolitionist movement**. His newspaper, *The Liberator*, first published in 1831, became the voice of those seeking an immediate end to slavery. Although Beecher opposed slavery, he believed that America's slavery problem was too complicated to resolve overnight. He supported the American Colonization Society's campaign to send blacks to Liberia, a new African nation created as a haven for former slaves. Garrison initially supported the colonization plan as well but soon abandoned it as a failure. He eventually came to believe that the plan served only those who wanted to eliminate blacks from America.

Missouri Compromise Debates

Harriet learned about abolition and the woes of slavery at an early age. When she was eight or nine, she heard family members discussing the debate in Congress over whether to allow Missouri to join the Union as a slave state. These early impressions, together with her religious training, convinced her that slavery was evil and against God's will. She later wrote to Frederick Douglass, a former slave and leading abolitionist, about her father's sermons on slavery during the Missouri controversy. Lyman Beecher's words instilled in her feelings against slavery so strong that she recalled his sermons thirty years after he preached them:

The Rev. Lyman Beecher, a dynamic speaker and passionate reformer, served congregations from Boston to Ohio for fifty years.

I was a child in 1821 [1819–1820], when the Missouri question was agitated & one of the strongest & deepest impressions on my mind were my father's sermons & prayers—& the anguish of his soul for the poor slave at that time—I remember his preaching drawing tears down the hardest faces of the old farmers—I remember his prayers night & morning in the family for "poor oppressed bleeding Africa" that the time for her deliverance in the family might come—prayers offered with strong crying & tears which indelibly impressed my heart & made me what I am from my soul the enemy of slavery …

Harriet was not the only one whose views of slavery were influenced by the "Missouri question." Until the debate over the Missouri Compromise in the early 1800s, most Southerners characterized slavery as a "necessary evil." They argued that they needed slaves to provide the labor required to produce the crops on which the nation's economy depended. But few defended slavery itself as a good practice.

That changed in 1818 when Congress considered whether Missouri should be accepted into the Union as a new state where slavery was permitted. By that time, Canada had outlawed slavery, and the New England states had banned it within their borders. Northern states without official sanctions would soon pass laws against slavery. Maine, which also had applied for statehood, fell under the jurisdiction of Massachusetts, where slavery had been illegal since 1783.

Most Northerners opposed adding new states that allowed slavery. At the time of the debate, the United States was divided equally between states that allowed slavery (slave states) and those that did not (free states). The Missouri Compromise, enacted in 1820, kept the balance by granting statehood to Missouri as a slave state and Maine as a free state.

During the debate that led to the compromise, Northerners noted that Southerners had always referred to slavery as a burden that they had to bear. Representative John W. Taylor of New York suggested that Southerners take the opportunity to rid themselves of such a "burden":

> Gentlemen have now an opportunity of putting their principles into practice. If they have tried slavery and found it a curse; if they desire to dissipate the gloom with which it covers their land; I call upon them to exclude it from the Territory in question [Missouri]; plant not its seeds in this uncorrupt soil …

Taylor's speech led Southerners in Congress to defend slavery. They told of contented slaves who loved their masters and enjoyed their work. During one debate, Senator William Smith of South Carolina went so far as to claim that slaves were happy to be enslaved:

> There is no class of laboring people in any country upon the globe, except the United States, that are better clothed, better fed, or are more cheerful, or labor less, or who are more happy, or, indeed, who have more liberty and indulgence, than the slaves of the Southern and Western States.

Harriet Tubman, conductor on the Underground Railroad

Real Truths about Slavery

There were landowners who treated their slaves relatively well. There were slaves who were fond of the white children they raised and in some cases their white masters. But the real story of slavery was far from the happy domestic scene painted by these Southern lawmakers. If slaves really had a life as good as the Southern senators claimed, why did so many try to escape? And once free, why didn't they return to their masters after the hard life they faced on their own?

Harriet Tubman, who guided dozens of slaves to freedom along the **Underground Railroad**, the secret path to freedom, once told an interviewer:

> I was not happy or contented: every time I saw a white man I was afraid of being carried away … Now I've been free, I know what a dreadful condition slavery is. I have seen hundreds of escaped slaves, but I never saw one who was willing to go back and be a slave.

Most slaveowners considered slaves to be a lower class of human. They held the view that these "subhumans" did not have the mental abilities whites possessed, did not have the same attachments to their children and other relatives, and needed to be "guided" by superior white masters. Even some Northerners who opposed slavery shared this view.

Plantation owners used these opinions to justify brutal treatment of slaves. They relied on whippings and other violent actions to "teach" slaves their duties. Photographs and firsthand testimony by slaves proved that they endured vicious whippings, beatings, and savage attacks by their owners. Even those who escaped such cruelty had to work from dawn to dusk, had no say over their lives or their families, and were barred by law from owning property.

Owners generally provided just enough care to keep slaves alive and healthy. Most slaves did not have

No. 5.

THE LASH.

a healthy diet. They ate cornmeal, peas, molasses, lard, flour, and occasionally, meat. Fresh greens and vegetables came from small gardens they grew near their cabins.

Slaves wore clothing provided by their masters. Children often went naked, and many slaves too old or sick to work did not have enough clothing to keep them warm in winter. Most slaves lived in shacks, though some who worked in the main house lived in spare rooms separate from the rest of the building.

In some states it was illegal to teach slaves to read and write. Even so, a number of slaves became literate on their own or were taught by their white masters.

Although slaves could marry, they had no guarantee that their husband or wife would not be sold and taken to another plantation or state. Children of slave mothers became the property of the master, who could sell them at will and at any age. Toddlers sold might never see their parents and siblings again.

"Slavery Is Damnable!"

Harriet Ann Jacobs, a slave on a North Carolina plantation who escaped and published an autobiography in 1861, described the agonies of an enslaved mother whose master sold her child:

> Could you have seen that mother clinging to her child, when they fastened the irons upon his wrists; could you have heard her heart-rending groans, and seen her bloodshot eyes wander wildly from face to face, vainly pleading for mercy; could you have witnessed that scene as I saw it, you would exclaim, *Slavery is damnable!*

For the first twelve years of her life, Jacobs lived with a caring white mistress, who taught her to read and sew. When the mistress died, however, Jacobs became

the property of a vile man who beat her and harassed her constantly. She escaped to her grandmother's cabin, where she lived in a tiny crawl space for seven years. When she finally escaped to freedom, she was forced to leave her two children behind. After years of separation, she reunited with her children in New York City.

Enslaved parents faced the agony of losing their children when they were sold to owners on faraway plantations.

Harriet Beecher Stowe and *Uncle Tom's Cabin*

A notice posted by James Norcom offers a reward of $100 for the return of his slave Harriet Jacobs. After being attacked and harassed by Norcom, Jacobs hid in a crawl space for years before escaping to the North.

Preaching on Paper

During her years as a writing teacher at the Hartford Female Seminary, Harriet developed skills in public speaking, studied drawing and painting, and became involved in national issues. Her father's religion and society in general frowned upon women who spoke publically before groups of men and women. Yet Harriet learned to deliver speeches before audiences of female students just as her brothers preached before their congregations. "I shall become quite an orator if you do not come home too soon," she wrote in a letter to Catharine after giving a speech during her sister's absence from the school.

Instead of becoming a preacher, as her father and brothers had done (a career barred to women), Harriet used her skill with words to "preach on paper." In a letter to her brother George in 1830, she wrote, "I was made for a preacher—indeed I can scarcely keep my letters from turning into sermons."

Introducing
Uncle Tom

When Harriet was twenty-one, in 1832 her father became president of Lane Theological Seminary and the family moved to Cincinnati, Ohio. Catharine founded a new school for women in Ohio, the Western Female Institute, and Harriet continued as a teacher there. At that time, in the early 1830s, Cincinnati was a bustling city with thirty thousand residents at the gateway to America's West.

Seeing a need for a geography book for children, Catharine asked Harriet to write one. Eager to have her work published, Harriet wrote *Primary Geography for Children*. The book, with maps and engravings, was written as a **narrative** (in the form of a story).

Catharine was listed as the author, most likely because of her credentials in the education field. But the title page gave credit to Harriet. The sisters split the proceeds from the book, which sold well.

Catharine and Harriet soon joined a literary group called the Semi-Colon Club. Group members read samples of their works aloud, discussed them, and encouraged each other's efforts.

One of Harriet's early readings, a humorous piece about a New England farmer, got a warm response from the club's members. After hearing the work, an editor who attended the Semi-Colon Club invited Harriet to enter the sketch in his magazine's fiction contest. She did and won the $50 prize and publication of her first fictional story, "A New England Sketch." Other sketches followed, and in 1843 she published a collection of the stories in her first book for adults, *The Mayflower*.

American readers, hungry for tales about ordinary people and experiences they shared, responded enthusiastically to Stowe's writings. Her snapshots of down-to-earth characters, humorous happenings, and realistic dialogue marked a major change in American literature. Until then, few American writers had published such intimate stories of everyday life. "At her best, Harriet Beecher Stowe was the first American **realist** of any consequence," said Milton Rugoff, biographer of the Beecher family.

Calvin Stowe and Harriet Beecher married in 1836 and supported each other for the next fifty years, until Calvin's death.

Harriet met new friends when Calvin Stowe joined the faculty at Lane. Lyman Beecher had been a mentor to Stowe in Boston and hired him to teach biblical literature at the seminary. Stowe, a noted scholar, and his young wife, Eliza, moved to Cincinnati in August 1833.

Eliza Stowe and Harriet soon became the best of friends. They spent much of their free time together. Eliza Stowe died in 1834 at the age of twenty-five during a cholera outbreak in Cincinnati. Harriet and Eliza's widower, Calvin Stowe, were heartbroken. Their grief drew them together. The couple married two years later. In January 1836, Harriet began her new life as Mrs. Harriet Beecher Stowe.

Theodore Weld, a passionate and fiery reformer, led the abolition effort in Ohio.

Protest and Violence

Shortly after their marriage, Calvin Stowe left on an extended tour of Europe. Harriet then moved to her father's house on the east side of Cincinnati. As the largest city in Ohio, a free state bordering the slave state of Kentucky, Cincinnati became a hotbed of unrest as abolitionists pushed for an end to slavery and proslavery forces reacted with increasing violence.

Theodore Weld, a student at Lane Seminary in the 1830s, became an activist and firebrand in the abolitionist cause. Weld would also play an important role in Stowe's eventual writing of *Uncle Tom's Cabin*. Stowe read Weld's 1839 book, *American Slavery As It Is*, which he based on reports in Southern newspapers. The book contained detailed evidence of the abuses heaped upon slaves and the violent acts of slaveholders. It became a best seller, with 100,000 copies sold during its first year of publication. The book helped focus attention on the evils of slavery and won new converts for the abolition movement. Stowe said later that she kept a copy of the book nearby as she wrote *Uncle Tom's Cabin*. Many of Weld's details served as a basis for events in Stowe's book.

As abolitionist protests increased, attacks and violence became commonplace in cities from Maryland to the Northeast. Mobs in Boston dragged abolitionist William Lloyd Garrison over cobblestone streets. Rioters in other cities focused on abolitionist newspapers. When James G. Birney, a former slaveholder turned abolitionist, brought his antislavery weekly, the *Philanthropist*, to Cincinnati, a mob broke into his office and damaged his printing press. Birney continued to print his antislavery pieces, and a second mob threw the press in the river and burned down several houses. Henry Ward Beecher responded to the mayor's plea and joined town leaders who armed themselves to disperse the mob. Harriet praised her brother's actions.

By then, most of the Beechers had taken strong stands in support of the abolition movement. The 1837 murder of Elijah Lovejoy, an abolitionist newspaperman and good friend of Harriet's brother Edward Beecher, sealed

An anti-abolition mob torches a warehouse and the printing press inside, which Elijah Lovejoy bought to produce his antislavery newspaper in Indiana in 1837. Lovejoy was shot and killed during the riot.

their determination to work against slavery. Edward signed on as manager of the Illinois Anti-Slavery Society. Henry gained national recognition as a powerful voice against slavery from the pulpit of New York's Plymouth Church. The church itself served as a stop on the Underground Railroad. As the conflict grew and tension between North and South escalated, Harriet Beecher Stowe would take pen in hand and lead her own battle against slavery.

"I Will Write"

For the next decade, Stowe was occupied with family duties. After giving birth to twins Eliza and Harriet, Stowe had five other children. The last child, Charles Edward, was born in Brunswick, Maine, where the family moved in 1850 when Professor Stowe accepted a position at Bowdoin College. Before the move, the Stowes buried their sixth child, eighteen-month-old Samuel Charles Stowe, a victim of cholera. About the tragedy, Harriet said, "It was at *his* dying bed, and at *his* grave that I learnt what a poor slave mother may feel when her child is torn away from her." She later shared that Samuel Charles's death served as an inspiration when she was writing *Uncle Tom's Cabin*.

During this time Stowe provided needed money for the growing family by writing regular pieces for a number of newspapers and journals. "If you see my name coming out everywhere—you may be sure of one thing, that I do it for the pay," she wrote to her friend Mary Dutton.

Stowe's name soon became familiar to readers of newspapers in Ohio, New York, and elsewhere. She wrote both fiction and nonfiction on a wide array of topics. She described a trip on a canal boat, praised her brother Henry's ability as a preacher, warned against the evils of alcohol and slavery, and wrote about the moral obligation to pay seamstresses decent wages. Her fiction—written with a light, humorous touch—focused on memorable characters who lived in rural New England. Her stories in *Godey's Lady's Book*, a popular women's magazine, introduced Harriet Beecher Stowe to thousands more readers. Her first submission to the magazine, "Trials of a Housekeeper," described a new wife's humorous struggles with a spectacularly incompetent maid:

> [O]ne week every pocket handkerchief in the house was starched so stiff that you might as well have carried an earthen plate in your pocket; the tumblers looked muddy; the plates were never washed clean or wiped dry unless I attended to each one; and as to eating and drinking, we experienced a variety that we had not before considered possible.

Even with the help of Calvin's mother and a hired woman, it was a challenge for Stowe to carve out time for writing. She described her hectic schedule after the family moved to Maine in a letter to her sister-in-law Sarah Beecher:

> [W]hen I look back, I wonder at myself, not that I forget any one thing that I should remember, but that I have remembered anything. From the time that I left

Cincinnati ... , it has seemed as if I could scarcely breathe, I was so pressed with care.

Nevertheless, Stowe managed to write daily for about three hours—on good days. She settled herself on the table near the big fireplace in her parlor and set to work.

In 1850, the same year the Stowes moved to Maine, an act of Congress set the country on edge, heating up the debate over slavery even more. The Fugitive Slave Act made it much harder for slaves to escape their owners. Not only did it increase penalties for those aiding fugitive slaves, it required Northerners to assist in their return. The new law also swept away legal protections for slaves and freed blacks. Many Northern states had required slaveholders to prove ownership before removing fugitives and had granted blacks accused of being runaways the right to a trial. Those guarantees no longer existed under the new law.

Reports of free blacks being kidnapped, **slave catchers** taking escaped slaves back to captivity, and falsified claims of slave ownership filled Northern newspapers. In Boston, officers seized Shadrach Minkins as he waited on tables at a local coffeehouse and jailed him at the courthouse. Minkins had escaped from the Virginia plantation where he was enslaved and had been living and working in Boston. Enraged abolitionists stormed the courthouse, freed him, and helped him escape to Canada. Similar episodes occurred in Syracuse, New York, and other Northern cities.

Isabella Beecher, now in Boston with husband Edward, wrote Stowe long letters describing the injustices taking place in that city. She urged her

SALES THIS DAY.

PURSUANT to an advertisement affixed to the door of the Court House of the city of Norfolk,

WILL BE SOLD,

At Public Auction, before the Court House, at 12 o'clock, on MONDAY, the 23d inst.,

Negro Man Shadrach and Negro Woman Hester and her children Jim and Imogene, by virtue of a writ of fieri facias against the goods and chattels of Martha Hutchings and Edward DeCormis, at suit of Joseph Cowperthwaite, assignee of the President, Directors & Co. of the Bank of the United States.

jy 18—tds ⠀⠀⠀⠀⠀ WM. B. LAMB, Serg't.

(Beacon copy.)

1849

A flyer announcing the sale of Shadrach Minkins spurred abolitionists in Boston to free him and help him escape to Canada.

sister-in-law to use her talents to expose the cruelties of slavery:

> Now, Hattie, if I could use a pen as you can, I would write something that would make this whole nation feel what an accursed thing slavery is.

Harriet, still caring for infant Charles, pledged, "I *will* write something." She had already written a sketch that was critical of the Fugitive Slave Act. The tale, about a farmer who refused to help fugitive slaves, was published in the *National Era*, a weekly Washington, DC, newspaper dedicated to abolition.

One Sunday in February 1851, as Stowe sat in church, she had a vision of an old slave being whipped to death because he refused to betray his fellow slaves. As he lay dying, the suffering man prayed to God to forgive his killers. When Stowe returned home, she wrote down the vision in the form of a sketch. Listening to a reading of the sketch, her children cried out against slavery. When Calvin Stowe read the piece, he urged his wife to write a longer version of the story.

Stowe asked the *National Era*'s editor, Gamaliel Bailey, if he would print "a series of sketches" she planned to write about slavery. Stowe estimated she would write three or four pieces in all. The series, as it turned out, ran weekly in the paper from June 5, 1851, to April 1, 1852.

Truth as Fiction

"Uncle Tom's Cabin; or Life Among the Lowly"—Stowe's title for the series—is the story of a noble, deeply religious slave named **Uncle Tom**, his various owners (kind and cruel), and other slaves he encounters. The tale opens with Tom's sale to a slave trader. Though his master, Arthur Shelby, a Kentucky farmer, has always treated slaves kindly, he sells Tom to pay his debts. Bought by a

Eva and Uncle Tom, two main characters in *Uncle Tom's Cabin*, pass the time together at the St. Clare plantation.

kind but weak master, Augustine St. Clare, Tom develops a fond relationship with St. Clare's little daughter, Eva. Her death convinces St. Clare to free Tom, but before he can fulfill his promise, he too dies. St. Clare's cruel widow sells Tom to a brutal slavemaster, Simon Legree, who owns a plantation in New Orleans. Beaten and mocked by Legree for his religion, Tom does not lose his faith in God. He encourages two slave women, Cassie and Emmeline, to escape from Legree's cruelty. When he refuses to reveal the women's whereabouts, Legree orders his overseers to beat Tom to death.

Who's Who in
Uncle Tom's Cabin

Uncle Tom Religious, moral, and noble slave, the novel's hero.

George Harris Inventor, slave owned by cruel master, Mr. Harris.

Eliza Harris Mrs. Shelby's slave; George's wife and **Harry**'s mother.

Arthur Shelby and his wife, **Emily**. Kentucky farmers who treat slaves kindly but sell Tom and Harry to slave trader **Dan Haley** to pay off debts.

George Shelby The Shelbys' son.

Aunt Chloe The Shelbys' cook, married to Tom.

Senator and Mrs. Bird The Ohio couple who help Eliza and Harry escape.

Simeon and Rachel Halliday Quakers who aid Eliza and Harry.

Augustine St. Clare New Orleans landowner who is opposed to slavery but enjoys the lifestyle it provides; married to **Marie St. Clare**.

Evangeline St. Clare ("Eva") Beautiful, good daughter of St. Clares who is fated to die.

Ophelia St. Clare St. Clare's cousin from Vermont.

Cassie Slave forced to become Legree's mistress; mother of Eliza. She escapes with another slave, **Emmeline**.

Topsy Mischievous slave girl owned by St. Clare and transformed by Eva's love.

Simon Legree Evil plantation owner who buys Tom at an auction.

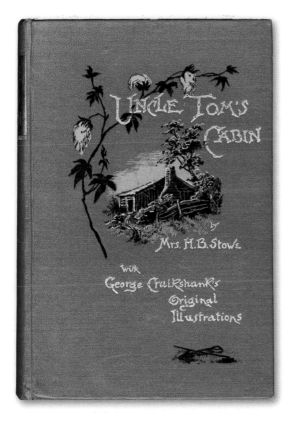

As he lies dying, Tom forgives Legree and his tormenters. His original master's son, George, arrives too late to buy Tom and return him to his plantation, where Tom's family awaits.

Another storyline follows Eliza, also the Shelbys' slave. She flees with her son after learning that the young boy will be sold along with Tom. She and her husband, also a fugitive slave, eventually reunite and are helped to freedom by Quakers and others. In Canada, they encounter Emmeline and Cassie, who turns out to be Eliza's long-lost mother. The family eventually moves to Liberia.

The story ends as George Shelby returns to his estate and frees his slaves to honor Tom's memory.

Stowe portrayed the slaves in her story as characters with feelings shared by the reader. She wrote about their love for their children, their pain of being separated from loved ones, their fear, and their faith in God. Stowe describes the terrified Eliza as she escapes with her little boy, followed by a passage inviting readers to imagine themselves in Eliza's situation:

But stronger than all was maternal love, wrought into a paroxysm of frenzy by the near approach of a fearful danger. Her boy was old enough to have walked by her side, and, in an indifferent case, she would only have led him by the hand; but now the bare thought of putting him out of her arms made her shudder …

If it were *your* Harry, mother, or your Willie, that were going to be torn from you by a brutal trader, tomorrow morning,—if you had seen the man, and heard that the papers were signed and delivered, and you had only from twelve o'clock till morning to make good your escape,—how fast could you walk? How many miles could you make in those few brief hours, with the darling at your bosom,—the little sleepy head on your shoulder,—the small, soft arms trustingly holding on to your neck?

Readers were enthralled with Stowe's first installments of the story. They asked for more, and Harriet found herself writing new chapters week after week. The *National Era* doubled its circulation during the series' publication.

Shortly before the last installment appeared in the newspaper, the Stowes agreed to a contract with Boston publisher John P. Jewett to publish the series as a book. The first books, published in two volumes, were released in March 1852. Harriet Beecher Stowe's three or four sketches had evolved into a 180,242-word book.

CHAPTER THREE

Truth and Lies

The March 1852 publication of Harriet Beecher Stowe's *Uncle Tom's Cabin* took America and Europe by storm. The first edition, ten thousand copies, sold out in three days. This was followed by several more printings. In the mid-1800s, long before television and radio, Americans read aloud from newspapers and books for entertainment. The *New York Times* estimated that if 100,000 books had been sold, "a half-million persons have read it." Sales during the first year topped 300,000 in the United States.

In two months, the book was available in London, where readers snapped up another million and a half copies. According to the *New York Times*, "*Uncle Tom's Cabin* is at every railway book-stall in England, and in every third traveller's hand." It eventually became the

best-selling **novel** of the nineteenth century. Only the Bible had more sales during that time. In 1879 the publishers announced that the book had been printed in more than thirty-seven languages.

In three months, Stowe earned $10,300 from sales of the book. The *New York Times* reported that it was believed to be "the largest sum of money received by any author, either American or European, from the actual sales of a single work in so short a period of time." The Stowes welcomed the money, which helped pay their living expenses.

The popularity of the book thrust Stowe into the spotlight as a major player in the abolition vs. slavery debate. Critical response was overwhelming, with reviews appearing in the *New York Times* and other prominent US papers as well as leading publications in England and the rest of Europe. At first reviewers in the North praised the work. But as hundreds of thousands of readers began to respond to the book, reviewers became increasingly critical.

Vicious Attacks and Book Bannings

Publications in the North as well as the South took Stowe to task for writing a book which they claimed "unnecessarily stirred up bitter feelings" around the slavery question. The *London Times,* in an editorial reprinted in many US newspapers, criticized Stowe for writing a book that "will keep ill-blood at boiling-point." The critics contended that slavery could not, and should not, be ended immediately:

> We do not believe that the blacks in America are prepared for sudden emancipation; and, if they are, we are certain that the whites are wholly incapable of appreciating the blessing. … [A]bolition must be the result of growth, not of revolution, must be patiently wrought out by means of the American Constitution, and not in bitter spite of it.

Southern attacks were more vicious. Critics there accused Stowe of twisting the truth, misleading readers about slavery, and damaging the reputation of slaveholders. Thomas Jefferson's grandson, Thomas Jefferson Randolph, called the book "a foul and atrocious Libel upon the slave holders of the Southern States, and … a garbage suited to the appetite of sectional hate."

The *Southern Quarterly Review,* in a lengthy review of the book, accused Stowe of possessing a "foul imagination which could invent such scenes" and "malignant bitterness" to create "an old addle thing, whose touch contaminates with its filth." The writer claimed that Stowe's fictional picture of slavery had no basis in fact.

Such attacks were repeated in pamphlets, newspapers, and religious tracts in the North and the South.

A painting that portrays slavery as an ideal condition for blacks in the South. The old slave gives thanks for the "massa," who pledges to do everything he can "to increase their comfort and happiness."

Several "anti-Uncle Tom" books appeared, filled with charming stories of happy slaves on Southern plantations—in sharp contrast to their life as portrayed by Stowe. The abolitionist newspaper the *Independent* published a review of one of these books, noting that it portrayed a life so pleasant that "one wonders why the inventors do not make haste to sell their children to the slave-traders."

Letters filled with obscenities and hate arrived at the Stowes' home. A cousin in Georgia told Harriet not to include the Stowe's name on the outside of letters Harriet wrote to her because she feared repercussions.

Officials banned the book in the South and passed laws making it illegal for blacks to own a copy. One free black preacher received a ten-year prison sentence for having a copy of the book in his house.

International Celebrity

Writing from her own perspective as a white woman, Stowe included stereotypes and assumptions about blacks in her book that would later be attacked as being racist. She romanticized her characters, making them too virtuous or too villainous. Little Eva is unbelievably good, as is Tom. Simon Legree, the cruel slavemaster who orders Tom beaten to death, is pure evil. Throughout the novel, Stowe inserted long passages on Christian doctrine and the immorality of slavery. These reflect one of Stowe's major themes in the book—that slavery violated Christianity and its teachings. Stowe believed Christians and their churches should lead the campaign to end slavery. A strong believer in Christianity, she hoped that Southern slaveowners would see that slavery was sinful and choose, on their own, to free their slaves.

However, it was Stowe's depictions of characters that people could relate to—not her preaching—that drew readers to *Uncle Tom's Cabin*. They cried when Tom and

Queen Victoria of England, one of the many readers of Stowe's *Uncle Tom's Cabin*

Eva died. They cheered when Eliza and Henry escaped to Canada. Stowe became a heroine—and international celebrity—to her readers. These included England's Queen Victoria, who received a copy of the book from the author herself.

In April 1853, the Stowes set sail aboard the steamship *Canada* for a ten-day voyage to Liverpool, England. It was the first overseas

Life as a Celebrity

The publication of a best seller thrust Harriet Beecher Stowe onto the international stage. She became a celebrity overnight. The British welcomed the author and her entourage with great enthusiasm. Thousands of men, women, and children stood alongside the docks to get a look at the famous American author as she disembarked from the steamship. The attention caught her by surprise:

> [M]uch to my astonishment, I found quite a crowd on the wharf, and we walked up to our carriage through a long lane of people, bowing, and looking very glad to see us. When I came to get into the hack it was surrounded by more faces than I could count. They stood very quietly, and looked very kindly, though evidently very much determined to look.

In the countryside, butchers, bakers, young mothers with children, ministers, innkeepers, and storekeepers smiled and bowed as she rode by. Even the servants in the home of the family with whom she stayed wanted a peek at the famous American author. At their request, she visited with the staff before continuing her travels.

trip for Harriet. Her brother Charles and his family accompanied the Stowes.

When they arrived, dukes, duchesses, earls, and bishops gathered at London's Stafford House to show their "respect and admiration" for Stowe. In sharp contrast to the elegantly attired members of the British aristocracy, Stowe wore a simple dress. A petite author, she could barely be seen among the lords and ladies. During the festivities Stowe accepted a petition from the women of England to the women of America calling for the end of slavery. It had been signed by half a million women in Great Britain and Ireland. The document appealed to their American sisters to do whatever they could to remove slavery from their land.

Bowing to the social custom of the time, Stowe declined to speak at events, relying on her brother and husband to do the talking. Everywhere she traveled, however, people had already read her words in the volumes of *Uncle Tom's Cabin*.

Charles Dickens

From England, she traveled to Scotland, France, Switzerland, and Germany, where fans lined the route and treated her like royalty. People brought bouquets of flowers and held up children to see the famous Mrs. Stowe. In Scotland the Stowes shared tea with two thousand people. In London they dined with author Charles Dickens and his wife, and met Elizabeth Barrett Browning and George Eliot. The Stowes returned to Europe again in 1856, where they saw Queen Victoria of England during a brief stop at a rail station.

Facts Behind Uncle Tom's Cabin

Just before her journey abroad, Stowe completed a book written in response to critics of *Uncle Tom's Cabin*. The work, *The Key to Uncle Tom's Cabin*, gave in great detail the facts upon which she based her fictional account. Readers bought copies of the new book almost as quickly as they had the novel. Some 60,000 copies of *The Key* were sold in three days' time. Sales eventually reached 150,000.

Stowe said she wrote her landmark book "because as a woman, as a mother, I was oppressed and broken-hearted with the sorrows and injustice I saw, because as a Christian I felt the dishonor to Christianity—because as a lover of my country, I trembled at the coming day of wrath." Stowe used *The Key* to rebut critics' charges that she had presented a false picture of slavery:

> This work, more, perhaps, than any other work of fiction that ever was written, has been a collection and arrangement of real incidents, of actions really performed, of words and expressions really uttered.

The Key told the story behind the story of Uncle Tom. In the book Stowe listed account after account of the brutal treatment of slaves, giving sources for each. She also included newspaper notices and articles, court testimony, interviews, and other documents.

Stowe had researched *Uncle Tom's Cabin* a number of ways. During her time in Ohio, she met slave owners and abolitionists, slaves, and former slaves. On a trip to Kentucky in 1834, Stowe visited a plantation, where

A flyer advertising a play production of *Uncle Tom's Cabin* and portraying the escape of Eliza and her son

she met a beautiful light-skinned woman who, she learned, was owned by the landowner. Stowe would later write that the knowledge that the young woman was a slave "struck a chill to her heart." The young slave would serve as Stowe's model for Eliza, one of the main characters in *Uncle Tom's Cabin*.

Before their marriage, Harriet and Calvin Stowe visited John Rankin, a minister who lived on the banks of the Ohio River, just across from Kentucky. Unlike Ohio, Kentucky was a slave state. During their stay, they learned that Rankin ran a safe house for slaves escaping from bondage. His house served as a stop along the Underground Railroad.

Rankin told of the harrowing escape of a young woman who fled with a baby in her arms across the ice-encrusted Ohio River to the safety of the minister's home.

He drove her to the next stop on the route to Canada. The tale of the young woman's escape made a lasting impression on Harriet. She later used the episode as a basis for one of the most dramatic scenes in *Uncle Tom's Cabin*: Eliza's escape across the icy Ohio River.

Other characters and scenes from Stowe's life found their way into the book. In 1839, the Stowes hired a young black woman as a servant. Professor Stowe helped the woman obtain legal documents acknowledging that she was a free woman. The Stowes learned that the woman's former master wanted to retrieve her and planned to snatch her if he could, despite the paperwork guaranteeing her freedom. The Stowes helped hide her until the danger passed. Later, when the family lived in Maine, the Stowes assisted a fugitive slave who sought shelter on the way to Canada.

While they lived in Ohio, Stowe and her husband hired a black woman named Eliza Buck as a cook and housekeeper. Eliza had been a slave to a brutal master in Louisiana, who was the father of her children. Stowe relied on Buck's accounts of slave life, including vicious beatings and indignities, to craft other scenes in *Uncle Tom's Cabin*.

The 1849 autobiography of Josiah Henson, which Stowe read, provided a model for Uncle Tom. Henson, a slave in Virginia, escaped to Canada after his master permanently injured his arms and reneged on an agreement to sell him his freedom. Self-educated, Henson became a preacher and lecturer and established a community for black refugees in Canada. Stowe also

Harriet Beecher Stowe used the story of Josiah Henson, pictured seated, as a model for Uncle Tom. Henson escaped from slavery in Virginia and went on to aid other freedom seekers.

borrowed scenes from the published works of Henry Bibb, an abolitionist and newspaperman who escaped from slavery on a Kentucky plantation, and from other slave stories in newspapers and magazines of the time.

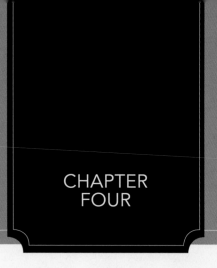

War and Beyond

Harriet Beecher Stowe's commitment to the abolition cause continued in the years after *Uncle Tom's Cabin* catapulted her to fame. In 1856, she wrote a second novel, *Dred, A Tale of the Great Dismal Swamp*. In it, she called for an immediate end to slavery.

In 1854, Congress passed the Kansas-Nebraska Act, which allowed voters in the territories of Kansas and Nebraska the right to choose for themselves whether to permit slavery on their lands. Stowe collected more than three thousand signatures from ministers in New England opposing the legislation. Southern clergymen, however, stood firmly behind the bill.

Soldiers capture radical abolitionist John Brown after he and his band attacked a federal arsenal in 1859.

The law's passage enraged abolitionists and set off acts of defiance that would soon plunge the nation into civil war. In 1859, John Brown led a small army of volunteers in an attack on the federal arsenal at Harper's Ferry, Virginia (later part of West Virginia). Brown and his band were captured and executed, but his example inspired others to fight passionately for abolition. In 1861, Confederate soldiers fired on Fort Sumter in Charleston harbor, South Carolina—the volley that started the Civil War.

In the years leading to the Civil War, Stowe devoted much of her time to earning a living and supporting her family with her writing. There were no international copyright laws, so she collected no **royalties**—payments made to authors—from European firms that published *Uncle Tom's Cabin*. Stowe became one of the first contributors to a new antislavery magazine, the *Atlantic Monthly*. The magazine featured the works of many of the leading literary giants of the time, poets Oliver Wendell Holmes Sr., James Russell Lowell, John Greenleaf Whittier, and Henry Wadsworth Longfellow among them.

After her busy European travels, Stowe settled in to her career as a famous writer. She wrote regular pieces for several publications and managed a household with children ranging in age from seven to twenty-one. Life seemed to be going well until nineteen-year-old Henry Ellis Stowe, Harriet and Calvin's oldest son, died in a drowning accident in New Hampshire near Dartmouth College, where he was a student.

His death, in 1857, left Stowe to wrestle with questions about the harsh, unforgiving form of Christianity preached by her father. Stowe explored some of those feelings in a third novel, *The Minister's Wooing*, the tale of a Puritan minister in New England, published in 1859. The book, which explored slavery in the North, first appeared as a serial in the *Atlantic Monthly*.

Believing Uncle Tom

Although the magazine took a strong antislavery stand, Stowe focused most of her pieces for the *Atlantic Monthly* on New England life and the type of characters she had developed in her earlier sketches. After the Civil War began, however, she used the pages of the magazine to call upon the women of Great Britain, who had once presented a petition to Stowe, to rally their own countrymen in support of the North in the Civil War:

> Sisters of England, think it not strange, if we bring back the words of your letter, not in bitterness, but in deepest sadness, and lay them down at your door … Sisters, what have *you* done, and what do you mean to do?

During the American Civil War, the British stayed neutral. England had strong ties to the South, which produced almost all the cotton that fed Britain's textile industry. When Northern blockades stopped the flow of cotton to the British mills, influential factory owners and investors sided with their Southern suppliers. Offsetting the push to aid the South was the strong antislavery sentiment among the British people. Stowe, for her part, had strengthened the resolve of the British against slavery with her book, *Uncle Tom's Cabin*. William Yancey, sent by the **Confederacy** in 1861 to assess British support for the South, wrote to a friend: "In the first place, important as cotton is, it is not King in Europe … The anti-Slavery sentiment is universal. *Uncle Tom's Cabin* has been read and believed."

In articles, sermons, and editorials, Stowe and her brother Henry Ward Beecher repeatedly urged President Lincoln to end slavery. Lincoln did not want to drive the **Border States** to join the Confederacy and so delayed action on the issue. As the war progressed and Northern troops made gains, Lincoln made plans to issue an order to free the slaves.

As the most famous minister of his time, Henry Ward Beecher preached against slavery from the pulpit of New York City's Plymouth Church.

Stowe wanted to see the president in person to be certain he intended to carry through with the order. The visit, in December 1862, did not last long, but Stowe left with the assurance that the president would keep his word. Lincoln delivered the **Emancipation Proclamation**, which freed the slaves in all the Confederate states, on January 1, 1863. It was during the visit that the president supposedly greeted Stowe with his comment that her book had started the war. Since there is no written record to confirm the quotation, many scholars do not believe that Lincoln actually said it. Some researchers describe the quotation as a humorous piece of family lore.

In 1864, the Stowes left their home in Andover, Massachusetts, where they had lived for a dozen years, and moved to Hartford, Connecticut. Harriet oversaw the construction of a mansion: her dream house financed with royalties from her writing.

Post-War Life

After the war, Stowe continued with her writing. During her lifetime, she wrote more than thirty books including several works for children, a collection of poetry, and countless character sketches, magazine articles, and essays.

In 1867, Harriet invested in a plantation in the South, mainly as a way of helping her son Frederick find useful work. She planned to employ newly freed blacks to operate the place, but the plantation soon failed. Frederick, the Stowe's troubled middle son, was wounded in the war and struggled with alcoholism. He disappeared in 1871 after traveling to California. While in Florida, Harriet bought a house, where the Stowes spent winters until Calvin's illness prevented their trips south.

With Calvin Stowe retired and the expense of maintaining their large house rising, the Stowes, in 1878, moved to a smaller house in Hartford, across the street from author Samuel Clemens, better known as Mark Twain. Stowe's last book, *Poganuc People*, was published that year. It recounted the stories she told so well of life in a New England parsonage. The writings were based on her own childhood.

Samuel Clemens, who wrote under the name of Mark Twain, lived across the street from the Stowes in Hartford, Connecticut.

In the next decade, Stowe lost several beloved family members. Calvin died in 1886, her brother Henry died a year later, and daughter Georgiana died in 1890. Stowe's youngest son, Charles, helped collect her letters and other materials into a biography. *The Life of Harriet Beecher Stowe* was published in 1889. Shortly afterward, Stowe lapsed

Paying Tribute

The signing of the Emancipation Proclamation brought about great celebrations throughout the North. The Stowes celebrated along with a huge crowd of abolitionists at the Boston Music Hall. The Grand Philharmonic Orchestra and a chorus entertained. Oliver Wendell Holmes, Ralph Waldo Emerson, Henry Wadsworth Longfellow, and a host of other literary and community dignitaries planned the event. Proceeds from the tickets, at one dollar or fifty cents, went to benefit freed slaves. By 10 p.m. the crowd was restless, waiting for news of the proclamation to be sent across telegraph wires. As the tension built, Emerson read his poem, "Boston Hymn," written for the occasion. Word finally came that Lincoln had signed the proclamation, and the crowd erupted with loud cheers, cries, and applause. Then someone spotted Harriet Beecher Stowe sitting in the balcony. She was a small, unremarkable woman of middle age draped in a shawl for warmth and wearing an old-fashioned bonnet over her curls. The crowd went wild, chanting, "Mrs. Stowe! Mrs. Stowe!" Silently, she rose from her seat and with tears flowing, accepted the crowd's admiration.

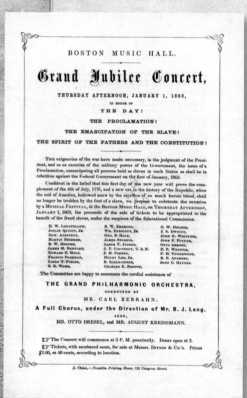

The program from the Grand Jubilee Concert celebrating the signing of the Emancipation Proclamation

Harriet Beecher Stowe and *Uncle Tom's Cabin*

into **dementia,** which affected her memory and mental abilities. As she herself described her condition in an 1893 letter to Oliver Wendell Holmes: "my brain is tired out." At times she was still sharp enough to write such letters and respond intelligently, but more and more she behaved as a child, wandering about the neighborhood and picking flowers. On July 1, 1896, she died in her sleep.

The *New York Times* marked the passing of "the authoress" of *Uncle Tom's Cabin* in a lengthy obituary on page five. The newspaper called her death "one of the closing leaves in an era of our century," noting she was "the writer of probably the most widely read work of fiction ever penned."

With the war long over and slavery in the past, Americans forgot the impact of *Uncle Tom's Cabin* on the national scene. Many knew Uncle Tom only from skits and plays that borrowed characters from Stowe's book. These productions began to appear as soon as *Uncle Tom's Cabin* became popular and continued to be offered through the 1900s. Stowe had no part in producing the shows and never saw her characters as they appeared on stage. While some early "Uncle Tom" plays portrayed the book more or less accurately, later versions changed the characters and storyline dramatically. Characters were greatly exaggerated and became humorous versions of those in the book. They relied heavily on **racial stereotypes,** which presented a false view of the qualities and behavior of black people based on their race.

Soon the productions evolved into musicals that centered on the happy life of slaves on the plantation and introduced comic characters with black faces designed to make audiences laugh. Often a white actor with his face painted black portrayed Uncle Tom and sang and danced his way through the show. In these productions, neither Uncle Tom nor Eva died, and abolition was not mentioned. These shows gave people a slanted and misleading view of the real meaning of *Uncle Tom's Cabin*. In time "Uncle Tom" became a term that meant a black person who willingly submitted to whites, even betrayed others of his race to win favor from whites of higher social standing.

Twentieth-century critics dismissed Stowe's writing as too sentimental and overly dramatic. They discounted her long passages about the glories of Christianity as outdated religious ramblings. Her characters, they said, lacked depth and were too good or too evil to be realistic. These critics objected to Stowe's black characters as racial stereotypes.

In a 1949 essay, James Baldwin, who became a leading American novelist and social commentator, wrote a scathing attack on Stowe and her book. He contended that Stowe unfairly stereotyped blacks by portraying them only as victims instead of showing them as real human beings. Baldwin called *Uncle Tom's Cabin* "a very bad novel" and berated Stowe for her **sentimentality**, which he called "the mark of dishonesty."

Civil rights activist and writer James Baldwin criticized the racial stereotypes in *Uncle Tom's Cabin*.

[S]he was not so much a novelist as an impassioned pamphleteer; her book was not intended to do anything more than prove that slavery was wrong …

In recent times, however, critics have rediscovered the importance of Stowe's contributions and have viewed the work in the context of the time in which it was written. Although some of the writing forms she followed are open to criticism, the effect of the work cannot be ignored.

The words of the *London Daily News*, describing Stowe's influence on world opinion, still ring true today. By writing *Uncle Tom's Cabin*, the newspaper said, Stowe revealed to the world the evils of slavery and persuaded millions of people to support the antislavery cause:

[S]he has been made, unintentionally and even unconsciously, the apostle of the greatest cause now existing in the world …

When she could bear it no longer, she spoke … She told, in the most straitforward way what happens every day in the slave States of America … The power of the book was in its truth.

"She was a rock-star figure at the time," said Maura Hallisey, a tour guide at the Harriet Beecher Stowe Center, the Hartford, Connecticut, museum devoted to the author and her works. "Stowe's words," the center notes, "changed the world: her bravery as she picked up her pen inspires us to believe in our own ability to effect positive change."

Chronology

Dates in green pertain to events discussed in this volume.

1619 The African slave trade begins in North America.

1777–1804 Slavery is abolished in the northern states.

1789 The US Constitution goes into effect.

1808 The foreign slave trade is abolished by Great Britain and the US.

1811 Harriet Elizabeth Beecher is born in Litchfield, Connecticut, to Lyman Beecher and Roxana Ward Foote Beecher.

1820 The Missouri Compromise requires northern states to help recapture fugitive slaves and allows slavery in the new state of Missouri and south of a line running along the southern border of Missouri. Lyman Beecher preaches against the expansion of slavery.

1833 The American Anti-Slavery Society is founded in Philadelphia.

1833–1834 Harriet's first published work, a geography textbook for children, is released. Her sister Catharine is listed as the author.

1836 Harriet marries Calvin Ellis Stowe, a widower and professor at Lane Theological Seminary. They live in Cincinnati near the college.

1836–1850 Harriet gives birth to seven children, three girls and four boys. Charley, the couple's sixth child, dies of cholera when he is eighteen months old.

1837–1839 The Grimké sisters speak against slavery to overflow audiences in New York and New England.

1843 Harriet's first book written under her own byline, *The Mayflower, Sketches of Scenes and Characters among the Descendants of the Puritans*, is published. She writes articles for two weekly papers in Cincinnati, the *Chronicle* and the *Journal*.

1849 Harriet Tubman escapes from slavery into Pennsylvania.

1850 US Congress passes the Fugitive Slave Act.

1851 *Uncle Tom's Cabin* runs as a serial in the abolitionist newspaper *National Era* in Washington, DC.

1852 Stowe's complete novel, *Uncle Tom's Cabin*, sells millions of copies.

1854 Congress approves the Kansas-Nebraska Act.

1855–1860 Harriet Tubman rescues freedom seekers and leads them from Maryland to Canada.

1856 Proslavery activists attack the antislavery town of Lawrence, Kansas; John Brown leads a raid on a proslavery family, which launches a three-month conflict known as "Bleeding Kansas."

1856–1878 Harriet continues writing novels, including a second antislavery book, *Dred: A Tale of the Great Dismal Swamp*.

1857 The US Supreme Court hands down decision in the *Dred Scott v. Sanford* case. Harriet and Calvin Stowe's son Henry drowns in the Connecticut River at age nineteen. Harriet Beecher Stowe's work is published in the first issue of the *Atlantic Monthly*. The antislavery magazine publishes her novel *The Minister's Wooing* as a serial.

1859 John Brown launches an attack at Harpers Ferry.

1860 Abraham Lincoln is elected president; South Carolina secedes from the Union.

1861 The Civil War begins.

1863 Lincoln's Emancipation Proclamation frees the slaves in Confederate-held territory.

1864 The Stowes move into a new house in Hartford, Connecticut, designed by Harriet.

1865 The Civil War ends. President Lincoln is assassinated. The Thirteenth Amendment to the US Constitution abolishes slavery.

1866 The American Equal Rights Association is formed. Its goals are to establish equal rights and win the vote for women and African Americans.

1868 The Fourteenth Amendment grants US citizenship to former slaves.

1870 The Fifteenth Amendment gives black men the right to vote.

1886 Calvin Stowe, Harriet's husband of fifty years, dies in Hartford, Connecticut.

1896 A group of black civil rights activists forms the National Association of Colored Women in Washington, DC. The group works to further civil rights for blacks and obtain the vote for women. Harriet Beecher Stowe dies at her home in Hartford, Connecticut.

Glossary

abolitionist An activist supporting the end of slavery.

abolitionist movement The campaign to ban slavery in the United States and elsewhere.

Border States Slave states that bordered free states before the Civil War.

Confederacy The government formed by the eleven southern states that withdrew from the United States during the Civil War.

dementia A condition that results in memory loss and a decline in mental abilities. Harriet Beecher Stowe suffered from dementia at the end of her life.

Emancipation Proclamation President Abraham Lincoln's order, in 1863, to free the slaves in the eleven states of the Confederacy.

free states States that banned slavery within their borders.

narrative A book or shorter piece written in the form of a story.

novel A fictional account of the lives of one or more characters.

plantation Large farms in the South, where cotton, rice, tobacco, or other crops were grown.

racial stereotype A false belief about the qualities and behavior of people based on their race.

realist In literature, a writer whose characters appear real and whose story and dialogue are true to life.

royalties Payments made to authors for their work.

slave catcher People paid to recapture runaway slaves.

slave states States that allowed slavery within their borders.

sentimentality Overly emotional; in literature, the use of too much sadness or emotion to stir feelings in a reader or listener.

Uncle Tom The lead character in Harriet Beecher Stowe's *Uncle Tom's Cabin*. In modern times, the term has come to mean a black person who is overeager to gain the approval of whites.

Underground Railroad The secret network of escape routes and safe houses leading from the South to freedom.

Union The states remaining as part of the United States during the Civil War.

Further Information

Books

Henson, Josiah. *Autobiography of Josiah Henson: An Inspiration for Harriet Beecher Stowe's Uncle Tom*. Seattle: Amazon (Kindle edition), 2012.

Rau, Dana Meachen. *Who Was Harriet Beecher Stowe?* New York: Grosset & Dunlap, 2015.

Sonneborn, Liz. *Harriet Beecher Stowe*. Leaders of the Civil War Era. New York: Chelsea House Publishers, 2009.

Stowe, Harriet Beecher. *Uncle Tom's Cabin: or Life Among the Lowly*. Carlisle, MA: Applewood Books, 2013.

Websites

American Slave Narratives: An Online Anthology
xroads.virginia.edu/~hyper/wpa/wpahome.html

This University of Virginia website offers first-person accounts of slavery by former slaves, including recordings of their actual voices. View photographs taken at the time of the interviews.

Harriet Beecher Stowe

xroads.virginia.edu/~ma97/riedy/hbs.html

The University of Virginia's American Studies website on Harriet Beecher Stowe includes links to excerpts and the complete text of *Uncle Tom's Cabin* and a selection of Stowe's letters.

Harriet Beecher Stowe Center

www.harrietbeecherstowecenter.org

This is a comprehensive site on Harriet Beecher Stowe, her family, and the effect *Uncle Tom's Cabin* had on US history.

Uncle Tom's Cabin & American Culture

utc.iath.virginia.edu

This site serves as University of Virginia's multimedia archive on *Uncle Tom's Cabin*. Included are songs, theater productions, responses to the book, and other related materials.

Bibliography

"American Slave Narratives: An Online Anthology."
University of Virginia. Accessed January 18, 2015.
http://xroads.virginia.edu/~hyper/wpa/wpahome.html.

American Slavery: English Opinion of "Uncle Tom's
Cabin." *New York Times*. September 18, 1852.
Accessed January 18, 2015. http://timesmachine.
nytimes.com/timesmachine/1852/09/18/87841925.
html?pageNumber=6.

Ashton, Susanna. "A Genuine Article." *Common-Place*.
13:4, summer 2013. Accessed January 18, 2015.
www.common-place.org/vol-13/no-04/ashton.

Belasco, Susan. "Harriet Beecher Stowe." *New York Times*.
Accessed January 18, 2015. http://topics.nytimes.com/
top/reference/timestopics/people/s/harriet_beecher_
stowe/index.html.

"Civil War." 150 Multimedia. Gilder Lehrman Institute
of American History. Accessed January 18, 2015.
http://www.gilderlehrman.org/civilwar150/multimedia.

"Four Days Later From Europe." *New York Times*.
May 25, 1853. Accessed January 18, 2015. http://
timesmachine.nytimes.com/timesmachine/1853/05/
25/87854488.html?pageNumber=3.

Gerson, Noel B. *Harriet Beecher Stowe: A Biography*.
New York: Praeger Publishers, 1976.

Giles, Waldron H. "Slavery and the American Economy." Accessed January 18, 2015. www.nathanielturner.com/slaveryandtheamericaneconomy.htm.

Gordon-Reed, Annette. "The Persuader: What Harriet Beecher Stowe Wrought." *New Yorker*, June 13, 2011.

Harriet Beecher Stowe Center. Accessed January 18, 2015. www.harrietbeecherstowecenter.org.

"Harriet Beecher Stowe Letters for the Years 1853 thru 1879." Familytales.org. Accessed January 18, 2015. http://www.familytales.org/results.php?tla=hbs.

"Harriet Beecher Stowe." University of Virginia. Accessed January 18, 2015. http://xroads.virginia.edu/~ma97/riedy/hbs.html.

"Harriet Beecher Stowe: *Uncle Tom's Cabin*." Gilder Lehrman Institute of American History. Accessed January 18, 2015. www.gilderlehrman.org/multimedia#!3264.

Harper, Douglas. "Slavery in the North." Accessed January 18, 2015. www.slavenorth.com/author.htm.

Hedrick, Joan D. *Harriet Beecher Stowe: A Life*. New York: Oxford University Press, 1994.

Bibliography

"News by the Mails." *New York Times*. July 12, 1852. Accessed January 18, 2015. http://timesmachine. nytimes.com/timesmachine/1852/07/12/74862257. html?pageNumber=2.

"Primary Documents in History." Accessed January 18, 2015. www.loc.gov/rr/program/bib/ourdocs/index.html.

"Proclamation of Emancipation, The." *New York Daily Tribune*. January 3, 1863. Accessed January 18, 2015. http://chroniclingamerica.loc.gov/lccn/sn83030213/1863-01-03/ed-1/seq-4.

Railton, Stephen, dir. "Uncle Tom's Cabin & American Culture." University of Virginia. Accessed January 18, 2015. http://utc.iath.virginia.edu.

Rugoff, Milton. *The Beechers: An American Family in the Nineteenth Century*. New York: Harper & Row, 1981.

Sklar, Kathryn Kish. "Victorian Women and Domestic Life: Mary Todd Lincoln, Elizabeth Cady Stanton, and Harriet Beecher Stowe." *Women and Power in History: Volume I to 1880*. Upper Saddle River, NJ: Prentice Hall, 2002. Accessed January 18, 2015. http://harvey. binghamton.edu/~hist266/week2/victorian.htm.

Stowe, Harriet Beecher. "Letter to Eliza Cabot Follen." December 16, 1852. London: Dr. William's Library. Cited in Hedrick, p. 193.

——. "Letter to George Beecher." February 20, 1830. Acquisitions, SD. Cited in Hedrick, p. 64.

——. "Letter to Mary Dutton," December 13, 1838. Mary Dutton-Beecher Letters, Bienecke Library, Yale University. Accessed January 18, 2015. http://harvey. binghamton.edu/~hist266/week2/victorian.htm.

——. *Key to Uncle Tom's Cabin*. Accessed January 18, 2015. http://utc.iath.virginia.edu/uncletom/key/kyhp.html.

——. *Uncle Tom's Cabin*. New York: Penguin American Library, 1981.

"Theodore Dwight Weld." National Abolition Hall of Fame and Museum. Accessed January 18, 2015. www. nationalabolitionhalloffameandmuseum.org/tweld.html.

"*Uncle Tom's Cabin* in Print: The Collection of Mary C. Schlosser." Vassar College Libraries. Accessed January 18, 2015. http://specialcollections.vassar.edu/exhibit-highlights/2001-2005/stowe.

"Unfounded Rumor, An." *New York Times*. May 31, 1852. Accessed January 18, 2015. http://timesmachine. nytimes.com/timesmachine/1852/05/31/75116458. html?pageNumber=2.

Index

Page numbers in **boldface** are illustrations. Entries in **boldface** are glossary terms.

About the Author

SUSAN DUDLEY GOLD is a writer, historian, editor, and graphic designer. She worked as a newspaper reporter and magazine editor before becoming a children's book author. She has written more than fifty books for middle- and high-school students on a wide range of topics. Her book on slavery and human rights, *United States v. Amistad: Slave Ship Mutiny* (Supreme Court Milestones), received a Carter G. Woodson Honor Book award. She has also written about slavery and civil rights in *Missouri Compromise* (Landmark Legislation), *Civil Rights Act of 1964* (Landmark Legislation), and *Brown v. Board of Education: Separate but Equal?* (Supreme Court Milestones). After serving a year as a VISTA volunteer, she currently manages a program to aid US veterans. She and her husband live in Maine, where they own a Web design and publishing company.